Teaching for Discipleship

Mike Carotta, EdD

Our Sunday Visitor Publishing Division
Our Sunday Visitor, Inc.
Huntington, Indiana 46750

Heintz, Ph.D.

_um_

_r_

. Rhoades
f Fort Wayne-South Bend
13, 2015

Nihil Obstat and _Imprimatur_ are official declarations that a book is free from doctrinal or moral
or. It is not implied that those who have granted the _Nihil Obstat_ and _Imprimatur_ agree with the
contents, opinions, or statements expressed.

ISBN: 978-1-61278-937-8 (Inventory No. T1710)
LCCN: 2015935280

Cover design: Lindsey Riesen
Cover art: Shutterstock
Interior design: Dianne Nelson

PRINTED IN THE UNITED STATES OF AMERICA

Table of Contents

Introduction

After a life in this work, the Church's call to teach for discipleship has made me more excited than ever before, and it is exactly what is needed at this time.

This book addresses several questions:

What is the Church's catechetical call to us and why does it make sense?

What are the challenges contained in this catechetical call?

How is it different than our past approaches?

What are some key characteristics of teaching for discipleship?

How might we sustain our ministerial commitment?

We carry the weight of the Church's catechetical hopes on our backs and in our hearts. It is good and noble work. I so hope that you find this book helpful and worth the read.

Our passion for this ministry sometimes fuels professional arguments about the correct way to approach catechetics. Critical reflection on our work is a good, constructive, and necessary thing. But sometimes ... not so much.

Working on her doctoral research several years ago, my wife, Cathy, showed me something the thirteenth-century Sufi mystic Rumi wrote:

> *Out beyond right doing and wrong doing*
> *there is a field.*
> *I will meet you there.*

I tried to write this book from that place.

PART I

THE CALL

Three major documents of the Church point to forming disciples as one of the principle goals for catechesis and evangelization — the *National Directory for Catechesis* (NDC), the *General Directory for Catechesis* (GDC), and *Renewing the Vision* (RTV).

The U.S. bishops tell us:

> Jesus formed disciples by making known to them the various dimensions of the Kingdom of God. He entrusted to them "the mysteries of the kingdom of heaven" (Mt 13:11); he taught them how to pray (Cf. Lk 11:2).... The fundamental task of catechesis is to achieve the same objective: the formation of disciples of Jesus Christ. Jesus instructed his disciples, he prayed with them, he showed them how to live, and he gave them his mission. (NDC, 20)

The Vatican tells us:

> Faith is a personal encounter with Jesus Christ, making of oneself a disciple of him. This demands a permanent commitment to think like him, to judge like him, and to live as he lived (Cf. CT, 20b). In this way, the believer unites himself to the community of disciples and appropriates the faith of the Church (Cf. CCC, 166-167). (GDC, 53)

7

And:

> The disciple of Jesus Christ deeply shares the "joys and hopes, the sadness and the anxieties of the men today" (GS, 1). He gazes upon human history and participates in it, not only from the standpoint of reason but also from that of faith. (GDC, 16)

And the U.S. bishops' Office of Laity, Marriage, Family Life, and Youth states:

> All ministry with adolescents must be directed toward presenting young people with the Good News of Jesus Christ and inviting and challenging them to become his disciples....
>
> We need to provide concrete ways by which the demands, excitement, and adventure of being a disciple of Jesus Christ can be personally experienced by adolescents — where they tax and test their resources and where they stretch their present capacities and skills to the limits. Young people need to have a true opportunity for exploring what discipleship ultimately involves. (RTV, Part Two)

Regardless of what age group you work with, this book offers some thoughts on the call, the challenge, and the differences found in teaching for discipleship.

But what is a disciple? And isn't a believer the same thing? Dr. Jeffrey Kaster points out:

> The Greek word for disciple, *mathetes*, literally means "learner" or "apprentice." The role of the Christian disciple is precisely to be a student or apprentice in the Christian way of life. (Assessing Christian Discipleship in Catholic

Youth Ministry, doctoral dissertation University of Minnesota, 2008)

And the Vatican reminds us:

The disciple of Jesus Christ is then ready to make an explicit, living, and fruitful profession of faith. (GDC, 56c)

Note how all these references define discipleship with broad strokes of the brush. This is how it should be. If we are not careful, we unconsciously further define discipleship so that it reflects our specific religious practices and spiritual interests. The recent interest in discipleship has resulted in various portraits of one who displays *specific* characteristics. I myself once came up with a list of characteristics describing the adolescent disciple. Let us leave discipleship as it came to us without adding more descriptions and characteristics. This is plenty good enough.

Nowadays I urge us to stay with the basic understanding that comes from the root word and the basic descriptions found in these catechetical documents of the Church — allowing for the variety of ways people live out the teaching of Christ.

The important thing that distinguishes the disciple from a believer is that *the disciple studies the ways of the One* throughout his or her life, and does his or her awful best to live life in accordance with those teachings.

By following the example of his self-giving love, we learn to be Christian disciples in our own time, place, and circumstances. (NDC, 29E; see also *Our Hearts Were Burning Within Us*, 46)

Why Now Is The Time

1. People already believe

Every religion poll in the United States over the last 20 years points to the same fact: almost 90% of Americans believe in God, believe in heaven and hell, and pray.

We are a nation of believers. And while fewer and fewer Americans actively participate in congregational life, they insist that religion still plays an important part in their lives.

Take, for example, the *Catholics in America* survey conducted in 2011 by researchers William D'Antonio of The Catholic University of America, Mary Gautier of Georgetown University, and Michelle Dillon, president of the Society for the Scientific Study of Religion. That study revealed that three out of four Catholics say the Church is important in their lives. The number is even higher among Hispanic Catholics.

The research found in *Souls in Transition: The Religious and Spiritual Lives of Emerging Adults*, by Christian Smith and Patricia Snell (Oxford University Press, 2009), reveals that while religious affiliation decreases among young adults after high school, the percentage of those who believe in life after death *increased* to 84%. The percentage among Catholic young adults was 88%.

In terms of Catholic identity among young adults:

- 81% say, "I have a lot of respect for organized religion."

- 72% say, "It is *not* a big turnoff for me."

- 77% say they have very positive feelings about being raised Catholic.

- 55% say that religion is *not* irrelevant to the needs and concerns of people their age.

- 66% say that there are too many religious people who are negative, angry, or judgmental.

- 71% believe many religions are true.

- 61% agree that you don't have to accept everything about Catholicism (an increase of 8%).

- 79% say you do not have to be involved in parish (up 12%).

- 71% say religion is a private matter and should be kept out of public debates and political issues.

- 49% expect to be attending religious services when they are thirty years old.

- 60% say that it is not important to marry someone of your religion; 14% say it is very important.

Smith and Snell point out, "We see little evidence of mass secularization among America's young adults except for a decline in regular church attendance" (102).

People already believe.

But according to these two researchers, the young are on "a trajectory" — not something as passive as a path or a journey — but a trajectory being propelled by multiple forces toward an adulthood wherein the influence of religion diminishes, practice of the faith declines, and engagement with the Church is minimal.

They maintain that this trajectory starts early: "It is not that what happens during teenage years and emerging adult years does not matter, it is simply that what matters even more is what happens before the teenage years, which powerfully conditions most everything that happens thereafter" (248).

So let's go back to the basic question: Can a person be a believer but not necessarily a disciple?

There is a difference between being a believer and being a disciple. A believer accepts some things about the existence and nature of God. A believer accepts a body of truth — most of which cannot be seen.

Being a believer is a strong step, something one should be proud of. And living out one's religious beliefs is the mark of integrity. Yet a believer is not the same thing as a disciple. One can be a believer but not necessarily a disciple.

Discipleship builds on belief. It is a way of inviting believers to the More. People today already believe. Discipleship is timely because it points believers to the More.

2. Religious faith is a common element of our culture

Flick the television remote and you will see:

- political candidates describing their religious upbringing and the importance faith plays in their lives today;

- winning athletes beginning post-game interviews by "giving Jesus Christ all the credit," or thanking "God for helping me today";

- ministers praying over congregational members, some slain in the spirit through the laying on of hands;

- a parish celebrating Mass;

- terrorists' attacks motivated by religious ideology.

We know the religious affiliations of our celebrities — who is a devout Catholic, a Scientologist, or a born-again evangelical.

Boomers grew up wondering if they would be "Touched by an Angel." A movie on the passion of Christ came out and millions of Americans from every denomination paid to go see it, even though it was in a language no longer spoken on the planet.

Religion is no longer something only discussed between the pulpit and the pew. It is in the commons of our culture.

3. Spiritual interests are high

Check out any week's New York Times' bestseller list and see how many of the top twenty paperbacks focus on spiritual topics. Sociologists tell us that the American people are pursuing spiritual interests at an unprecedented rate.

More Americans than ever actively practice yoga and other forms of meditation as a way to address both spiritual health and physical needs. Hospitals, health care networks, coffee shops, grocery stores, spas, and gyms now pitch themselves as ways to nurture body, mind, and spirit. Not only are we a nation of believers, people are drawn to topics and activities they view as spiritual.

4. The Call of Discipleship unites us

For those of us committed to faith formation, the Call of Discipleship transcends our particular theological interests, doctrinal emphasis, or political issues. It offers us a common purpose that we can all say yes to. It ends the kind of battles we have had with one another when we insist that the catechetical topic burning within our hearts should trump the ones burning in the hearts of others.

Yet, this call still allows each of us to pursue our favorite religious theme, social reform, or moral issue while seeing it as a contribution to a higher goal: discipleship.

The Call of Discipleship doesn't just unite catechists, it unites believers who come with different religious interests, questions, devotions, and perspectives. The Call of Discipleship provides a common purpose while leaving room for the diverse spiritual interests and practices of God's children.

5. Intentionality

The Call of Discipleship brings clarity to our work and cleans up the ambiguity found in too many of our current faith formation initiatives. It allows us to distinguish between basic formation and something More.

Teaching for Discipleship honors the necessary work of basic formation and then intentionally builds on it. We will see that it requires a different set of skills and has a different purpose. Some of us are more natural at T4D (teaching for discipleship) while some of us are better suited for the important work of basic formation.

6. Discipleship requires study and application

We know that the root word for disciple is *student*. By definition, a disciple is someone who studies the ways of the One and lives by them. It is more like a spiritual path than a spiritual level of achievement.

You can't be a disciple without *study*. It is a spiritual path one uses to direct one's life and navigate through. It is the challenging path and a noble adventure that Christ describes. It is a path that requires lifelong learning and constant application. On it, we take two steps forward and one step backward. Sometimes we rest; sometimes we lose our way.

And let us make this clear: *it is a path that comes with a cost.*

This goes against the trend to develop a basic collection of beliefs early in life — without study — or to form beliefs and then stop studying. This goes against mentally accepting a collection of beliefs without the active commitment to apply them.

7. Places community in context

Newsweek/Beliefnet surveyed 1,000 religious adults who identified themselves as "traditional" or "non-traditional" evangelical, Lutheran, Catholic, Methodist, etc. Approximately 275 were Catholic. Here's one question:

Which of the following would you say is the main reason you practice your religion (among traditional and non-traditional practitioners)?

	Trad.	Non-Trad.	Total
To forge a personal relationship with God	44%	28%	39%
To help you be a better person and live a moral life	31%	27%	30%
To find happiness and peace of mind	17%	17%	17%
To connect with something larger than yourself	10%	9%	10%
To give your life meaning and structure	8%	11%	8%

	Trad.	Non-Trad.	Total
To be a part of a community	3%	3%	3%
Other reason	1%	0%	1%
No main reason	5%	19%	10%
Don't know	2%	1%	2%

We see that the top three reasons people practice their religion corresponds to the vertical, horizontal, and internal dimensions of their spiritual lives. They practice their religion because it mainly helps them improve their relationship with the transcendent God, treat others lovingly, and find peace. (There will be more on these three dimensions in Part Four.)

But how many traditional and non-traditional members of these denominations practice their religion for community? 3%.

I did a workshop on T4D in a diocese recently with the local bishop in attendance. Before the workshop began, I approached him quietly with a request: "Bishop, I could really use some feedback on this stuff. Would you be kind enough to give this material a thorough theological evaluation?" He agreed to do it and said we could discuss it together with his diocesan staff at lunch afterward.

During lunch he pulled out an envelope from the inside pocket of his jacket. He had several points scribbled on the back of the envelope. We went through them. (To my joy, they were all positive.)

I asked him about the Newsweek/Beliefnet poll above. His response was immediate:

> That's what I hope people would say! For Pete's sake, people shouldn't be practicing their religion for community. They should be practicing it because of their love of God and faith in Christ. Not community!

While spiritual interests and pursuits among people in the United States increases at a record pace, congregational membership is dropping at a record pace. People are not in it for community. Even traditional members of our faith are not in it for community. Yet for the past two generations now, we have made community the focal point of our call to faith.

For the last thirty years, we have emphasized communal participation in our churches so much that it seems to be the principal indicator of faith. Communal participation and active membership seems to be the most important thing. We expect more and more of people as resources and talents of our churches dwindle while the need of our churches increase. We amp up the exhortations. Frustration increases. And so does the exodus.

The people have already voted with their feet. They ain't coming, ain't investing, ain't participating, ain't playin'.

They are not in it for community, which is all the more reason why now is the time for the Call of Discipleship.

Discipleship is a natural fit for the spiritual interests of the day because discipleship is first and foremost an individual act, not a communal one. At its most basic level, discipleship requires that an individual decide to study the ways of Christ and apply it to his or her life. It's a path with an easy on-ramp: making a personal commitment.

To me, the bishop mentioned above was echoing the words of Christ, who said clearly, and simply, "Stay in my word and you will be my disciples, and you will know the truth, and the truth will set you free."

But the Call of Discipleship is best nourished and lived out in community. Christ intentionally established the Church as the community of disciples. He called Peter to lead it.

The Call of Discipleship does not dismiss community. It places community in context.

It names the purpose of community.

We believe that *discipleship is best lived out within a community of disciples* — the Church. After all, "Where two or three of you are gathered, there I will also be" (see Mt 18:20).

The Vatican's *General Directory for Catechesis* says as much:

> In the Christian community the disciples of Jesus Christ are nourished at the two fold table: "that of the word of God and that of the Body of Christ" (DV, 21). (70)

> Jesus shows, equally, that the community of his disciples, the Church, "is, on earth, the seed and the beginning of that Kingdom" (LG, 5), and, like leaven in the dough, what she desires is that the Kingdom of God grow in the world like a great tree, giving shelter to all peoples and cultures. "The Church is effectively and concretely at the service of the Kingdom" (RM, 20). (102)

The Call of Discipleship simply changes the emphasis of our past approach without losing any elements of it. Instead of making community the principal focus from which one might pursue the spiritual life, it makes the individual act of discipleship the focus and presents community as the best way to support that life.

The same two elements of individual decision and communal membership remain — neither is lost. Yet the emphasis corresponds more directly to the spirituality of people today. This is one of the ways T4D is different than our past approaches.

8. Resonates with people's desire to help others

From tsunami relief to earthquake relief, from donating for malaria-preventing mosquito nets to celebrity-driven causes, from Going Green to Doctors without Borders, the moral imagination of the American people and its children is engaged when they are asked to make the world a better place.

T4D has a courageous and compassionate horizontal focus, not just a vertical or internal one. Author Leisa Anslinger often points out that when her parish in Columbus, Ohio, intentionally switched its focus to discipleship, the staff was able to document how the people responded: volunteerism exploded, donations rose, the number of ministries expanded, and the number of people subsequently engaged in communal membership increased exponentially.

The Call of Discipleship shifts from "support the parish" as the *primary* expression of the disciple's charity and compassion. The Vatican tells us:

> The community of the disciples of Jesus, the Church, shares today the same sensitivity as the Master himself showed them. With great sorrow she turns her attention to those "peoples who, as we all know, are striving with all their power and energy to overcome all the circumstances which compel them to live on the border line of existence: hunger, chronic epidemics, illiteracy, poverty, injustice between nations ... economic and cultural neocolonialism" (EN, 30)....
>
> "The church is duty bound — as her bishops have insisted — to proclaim liberation of these hundreds of

millions of people … of bearing witness on its behalf and of assuring its full development" (EN, 30). (GDC, 103)

Over the last eight years I have carved out a phrase that captures and connects the Call of Discipleship as I see it laid out in the Gospel, the documents of the Church, and the spiritual interests of the people. This phrase embodies the Call of Discipleship in a way that makes us touch all the bases on the way Home. Teaching for Discipleship also allows us to stop at any of the four bases and spend time probing the beauty and richness and truth there. Yet no single base captures all of it. T4D intentionally asks participants to touch all four bases on the way Home.

Discipleship …
> *within a community of disciples …*
>> *for the good of the world …*
>>> *and the will of God.*

For Reflection

How have you understood the word *disciple*?

This chapter lists eight reasons why now is a good time to emphasize the Call of Discipleship. Which one(s) do you agree with most and why?

Which one(s), if any, do you wish you could discuss a bit more?

What additional reason(s) might you want to add?

This chapter concludes with a statement that organizes and frames the Call of Discipleship. How does this sit with you?

Which of the four components have you been emphasizing in your own teaching?

Which might you want to increase your emphasis on?

Make yourself some notes about the one or two things you take away most from this chapter.

PART 2

THE CHALLENGE

FOUR WORDS

The Community of Faith

We have used these four words as a rich way to describe the Church. The Community of Faith implies a committed and dedicated body of people who are known for the faith they uphold and preserve. It is a diverse group of people who share the same beliefs, prayers, symbols, rituals, traditions, and morals.

Our Community of Faith is a Eucharistic one. At its best, the Community of Faith offers spiritual food for those who hunger, compassion for those in need, moral direction in a complex world, and spiritual wisdom for those who seek.

It has done so for 2,000 years.

faith of the community

Same four words, but a different reality. This represents the beliefs, morals, and spiritual guidelines of a larger group — many of whom may be full members of the Community of Faith but seem to resonate more with those in the larger public community.

Faith within these two different communities can often be very different, sometimes even opposed to each other.

What are the differences between the Community of Faith and faith of the community? And how are we to proceed?

Herein lays the biggest challenge in Teaching for Discipleship. The Vatican tells us:

> One of the difficulties to be addressed and resolved is the question of "language" (mentality, sensibility, tastes, style, vocabulary) between young people and the Church (catechesis, catechists). A necessary "adaptation of catechesis to young people" is urged, in order to translate into their terms "the message of Jesus with patience and wisdom and without betrayal" (CT, 40). (GDC, 185)

Given that those who were young people in 1997 (the year the *General Directory for Catechesis* was published) are now in their thirties, this "necessary adaptation" applies to our ministry among adults as well. And this Vatican document describes language as far more than vocabulary. It says that word language also refers to "mentality, sensibility, tastes, style" as well.

How are we to "translate … 'without betrayal' "?

Here are some of the differences in the "mentality, sensibility, tastes, style" that exist between the Community of Faith and faith of the community.

The Community of Faith	*faith of the community*
Sacramental Economy	**Existential Economy**
Christ manifests, makes present, and communicates his work through the liturgy of his Church (see Catechism of the Catholic Church, 1076). Grace is a free gift	Christ is found in the experiences of life. Grace is a free gift that is discovered.

The Community of Faith	*faith of the community*

mediated through the
sacramental life of the
Church.

**Topics Between
Pulpit and Pew**
Spiritual matters
are explored and taught
in church on Sunday.

**The Public and the
Commons**
Spiritual matters are
commonly shared on
television, in music, movies,
politics, sports, magazines.

**Invest in the
Parish**
Develop and maintain
the parish as the essential
source of spiritual strength.

**Invest in the Company
They Keep**
Develop and maintain
relationships for
strength.

Prefer *Our* Way
A commitment to
Catholicism as the
authentic expression of
the Christian faith
instituted by Christ and
passed on by the apostles.

Prefer Many Ways
A personal commitment
combined with a public
affirmation of all other
traditions, religious practices,
and movements.

**Hierarchy of Truths,
Ordered**
A core set of essential truths
that is the foundation

**Eclectic, Patched
Quilt**
A combination of beliefs
selected by the individual,

The Community of Faith	*faith of the community*
upon which other beliefs are built.	rejecting those that one does not agree with — even essential truths.

Sermons
Formal proclamation of the Word with care given to the historical background, information, or details with liturgical and moral implications.

Sound Bites
Preference for a simple synopsis without background information or details. Want a paragraph, not a page. Want the message in three minutes, not thirteen.

Theological Language
Appreciation for and use of the proper terms established to describe key concepts/ elements of the Tradition.

Plain English
Desire for simplicity in meaning of key concepts/ elements. No terms that require another level of understanding.

Moral Map
Specific teachings about specific moral issues and situations that one will encounter in life.

Moral Compass
Catholic moral principles that can be used to figure out right/wrong and be applied to all situations and issues.

Truth Revealed by God, Tradition
Upholding of revelation as found in the Scriptures and Church teachings.

Truth Found in Stories, Song
Cherishing illumination/ validation found in narrative, music, cinema.

The Community of Faith	*faith of the community*
Liturgical Calendar Rhythm of spiritual life and secular life guided by Church seasons.	**School Calendar** Rhythm of life guided by athletic seasons, parenting tasks.
Objective Morality Some things are wrong by their very nature — flat-out wrong.	**Moral Relativism** Depends on whether or not you think it is wrong. If you really think it's okay, then okay.
Accountability We are commanded to live a certain way. The Church is a source of moral guidance and leadership.	**Accommodation** We should try to understand everyone's choices. God understands. Stop judging. "Can't we all just get along."
Marinated Catholic Grew up practicing the faith, engaged with the parish, influenced by teachings. Swimming in it.	**Beige** Catholic without details or complexity. Be Catholic in a way that is neutral, warm, simplistic, compatible with other faiths.
Participation Sees active participation in the Church as the sign of one's commitment and faith.	**Identification** Sees calling oneself Catholic in the midst of religious diversity the sign of commitment.

The Community of Faith	*faith of the community*
Doctrinal Expression Values an acceptance of Creed and doctrines of the Church.	**Post-Doctrinal** Sees doctrine and creedal statements as unnecessary details and sources of division.
Transcends Culture Guided by "things of God."	**Shaped by Culture** Guided by cultural trends, cultural values.
Serve the Parish Parish should be the recipient of one's call to serve.	**Serve the World, "Cultureligion"** Less fortunate should be the focus on one's call to serve.
Emphasize the Knowing Knowledge of the faith is essential and should be a priority.	**Emphasize the Doing** Compassion for others and the way faith guides your life is all that matters.

So here is a major challenge in *Teaching for Discipleship*. How are we to make the "necessary 'adaptation of catechesis'" that can respond to the differences between the Community of Faith and faith of the community "*without betrayal*"?

The Church reminds us:

Catechesis must transmit the Gospel message in its integrity and purity. Jesus proclaimed the Gospel integrally ... "because I have made known to you all that I have heard from my father" (Jn 15:15). This same integrity is demanded by Christ of his disciples ... "teaching them to observe all that I have commanded you" (Mt 28:19). A fundamental principle of catechesis, therefore, is that of safeguarding the integrity of the message and avoiding any partial or distorted presentation ... "a disciple of Christ has the right to receive 'the words of faith,' not in mutilated, falsified or diminished form, but whole and entire, in all its rigor and vigor" (CT, 30). (GDC, 111)

Five sentences later the *General Directory for Catechesis* states. "Integrity must also be accompanied by adaptation" (112). This adaptation is shaped "in accordance with the capacity of those being catechized and the proper character of catechesis." In the same paragraph, in what might be the biggest understatement in the entire document, it says, "There is always tension in this necessary task."

BEIGE

I once heard Bishop Richard Malone, the current bishop of Buffalo, New York, describe modern-day Catholics as beige. This has always stuck with me. We paint the walls of our house beige because it "goes with anything." Beige is "neutral," accommodating all the other diverse colors.

So it is with beige belief. Beige believers want to be warm and accommodating to the various beliefs of others, even if it means that their own faith will lack detail ("colors"), practices, or characteristics that distinguish their religious identity from any of the others.

I once created a beige creed in one of my confirmation resources, *Have Faith*, to be critiqued in light of the Nicene Creed. The beige — or modern — creed might look like this:

Nicene Creed	modern Creed
I believe in one God, the Father almighty, maker of heaven and earth, of all things visible and invisible.	I believe in God whose Spirit is in everyone and everything.
I believe in one Lord Jesus Christ, the Only Begotten Son of God, born of the Father before all ages.	I believe in Jesus who was a son of God.
God from God, Light from Light, true God from true God, begotten, not made, consubstantial with the Father; through him all things were made. For us men and for our salvation he came down from heaven, and by the Holy Spirit was incarnate of the Virgin Mary, and became man.	
For our sake he was crucified under Pontius Pilate, he suffered death and was buried, and rose again on the third day in accordance with the Scriptures. He ascended into heaven and is seated at the right hand of the Father.	He taught us the ways of God and they killed him for what he taught.

Nicene Creed	modern Creed
He will come again in glory to judge the living and the dead and his kingdom will have no end.	He has an honored place in heaven again, with God.
I believe in the Holy Spirit, the Lord, the giver of life, who proceeds from the Father and the Son, who with the Father and the Son is adored and glorified, who has spoken through the prophets.	I believe in God's Spirit which is a good force in the world, helping everyone get through life.
I believe in one, holy, catholic, and apostolic Church. I confess one baptism for the forgiveness of sins and I look forward to the resurrection of the dead and the life of the world to come. Amen.	And I believe in heaven where I will see God after life.

What strikes you most about the beige creed? How would you describe it?

Part of the challenge in *Teaching for Discipleship* lies in *respectfully* pointing beige belief to the More, reintroducing Catholic young and old to the rich textures, layers, multicolored facets, complexities, and spiritual practices of the Tradition established by the Community of Faith for the life of discipleship.

We are reminded by the documents of the Church:

> Catechesis aims to foster development in all the distinct yet complementary aspects of the Catholic faith, for each one is a dimension of Christian discipleship. "The maturation of the Christian life requires that it be cultivated in all its dimensions: knowledge of the faith, liturgical life, moral formation, prayer, belonging to community, missionary spirit. When catechesis omits one if these elements, the Christian faith does not attain full development" (GDC, 87). (NDC, 48A3)

Teaching for Discipleship takes on the challenge to make a "necessary adaptation" to the way we engage in these catechetical tasks "without betrayal" instead of ignoring the responsibility to do so, cursing the existence of the gap between the Community of Faith and faith of the community, or blaming one group or the other for it.

THE CHEF AND THE COOK

Now and then I will ask a roomful of 100 people in a workshop to please stand if they considered themselves to be a cook — either a backyard cook, a household cook, or a professional cook. More than half of the room stands up. I then ask, "How many of you are chefs?" Everyone sits down — even the restaurant cook. Someone occasionally remains standing: a trained chef, retired.

Cook and chef. We don't use these titles interchangeably. What's the difference between a chef and a cook? Both can be great at cooking.

- A chef is the product of rigorous study and testing in culinary school or restaurant kitchens. Being a cook doesn't require the same amount or type of study and training. You can be a cook without serious study and testing, but you can't be a chef without serious study and apprenticeship.

- A chef has basic knowledge about *almost everything* related to cooking — that is, mother sauces; food temp; taste versus flavor; key traits of French, Asian, Creole cuisine; proper terms; parts of each animal, etc. A cook on the other hand knows about things related to his or her particular emphasis.

- A chef has developed proven skills with a variety of methods and techniques — that is, braise, broil, roast, sauté, poach, direct heat, indirect heat, marinate, emulsify, etc. A cook usually has skill at her or his favorite method(s).

- A chef knows when and how to use the appropriate method of cooking depending on the ingredients, environment, age of those being served, and desired results.

- A chef is evaluated regularly by customers, supervisor, general manager, colleagues. Whether weighty evaluations or casual ones, evaluations are normal to a chef. There are standards. A cook may or may not be evaluated often or with the same weight.

- When things are not working, a chef makes proper adjustments quickly and with confidence. A cook may or may not know how to adjust properly when things are not working, depending on their amount of study, skill, experience.

- A chef can tell ahead of time when a recipe is not going to work or the desired outcome is unrealistic — that is, "can't combine this with that"; "won't have enough time to cook all these things in an hour, especially if we use this method instead of that."

- A chef knows the exact dimensions of cooking that are his/her strengths and weaknesses. Knows exactly what they don't know enough about. A cook may or may not know what he or she doesn't know.

Do you have to be a chef in order to have good cooking? Heck no. Cooks make great meals without being chefs. A great cook can do better cooking than a weak or overly technical chef. A chef that approaches cooking in a highly technical way usually does not satisfy the hunger of those being served.

In fact, it is much more enjoyable to be fed by a cook who loves being with people than by a chef that does not seem to enjoy people.

But there is a question I'd like us to ponder for a second: What would happen if no cook ever aspired to become a chef and eventually we had no more chefs? How would that impact cooking and the culinary field?

Now, for a minute,
change cooking to catechetics,
change cook to catechist
change chef to religious educator,
and see where it takes us.

The "cooking" in catechetical ministry today is carried on the backs of volunteer catechists, or *cooks,* who love what they do and the people they serve.

As catechists, we bring our skill and passion to catechesis as full-time workers, part-time volunteers, certified and uncertified, just like cooks who feed people as backyard grill masters, household cooks, or paid restaurant professionals.

But there is a difference between a person "cooking" in catechetics as a catechist and one who is cooking in catechetics as a religious educator. Both can do catechesis quite well. But there is a difference.

- A religious educator is the product of disciplined study and testing. You can be a catechist without disciplined study and testing, but you can't be a religious educator without it.

- A religious educator has basic knowledge about *almost everything* related to catechetics. A catechist has knowledge about his or her particular catechetical offering.

- A religious educator has developed skills with a variety of methods and techniques. A catechist may have skill with her or his favorite method(s).

- Religious educators know when and how to use the appropriate method of catechetics depending on the material, environment, age of those being served, and desired end results.

- A religious educator is evaluated regularly by participants, colleagues, and supervisor — the evaluation has weight and effects one's reputation, if nothing else. A catechist may or not be evaluated often or with the same weight.

- When something isn't working, a religious educator changes catechetical methods with confidence. A catechist may or may not know how to adjust when something is not working, depending on the amount of his or her study, tested skills, experience.

- A religious educator can tell ahead of time when a lesson plan is not going to work or the desired outcome is unrealistic — that is, "can't combine this with that"; "can't address all these things in an hour"; "our kids won't be able to digest this."

- A religious educator knows exactly what catechetical skills and knowledge they lack. A catechist may or may not know what he or she doesn't know.

Let's be clear:

- Both catechists and religious educators can offer great catechesis.

- A great catechist can do better than a weak religious educator.

- A religious educator who approaches catechesis in a highly technical way does not satisfy the hungers of those being served. He or she can give religious educators a bad name.

- And it is more fun, *more memorable*, to be fed by a catechist that loves being with people than a religious educator who doesn't seem to enjoy people very much.

Catechists do some great cooking and have found ways to feed us well, without becoming a trained religious educator.

Not every catechist needs to become a religious educator. Not every cook needs to become a chef.

But suppose no catechist ever aspires to become a religious educator, and eventually we no longer have trained and talented religious educators? Won't that hurt the quality of catechetics just like the disappearance of chefs would hurt the culinary field?

Julia Child and modern **chefs encouraged us to be cooks and showed us how**. Cooking was energized. Today, we all learn from chefs, and the quality of cooking at home, in the backyard, and in restaurants continues to improve. And a new generation of cooks aspires to become chefs.

Father Johannes Hofinger, S.J., Maria Harris, Christiane Brusselmans, and other **religious educators encouraged us to be catechists and showed us how.** Catechesis was energized. But today, religious educators — the chefs of catechesis — are disappearing. And a new generation of catechists no longer aspires to become religious educators — or knows how.

That is one of the challenges we face.

It is a noble calling to noble work. It requires training, testing, study, and sacrifice. And those who come to our catechetical tables deserve spiritual sustenance cooked with grace, technique, taste, purpose, and care. They deserve the kind of cooking that makes catechesis a memorable experience.

For Reflection

What strikes you most about the differences between the Community of Faith and faith of the community?

What additional differences would you add?

Which "necessary adaptations" represent the biggest challenge(s) to your teaching style?

How would you sum up the difference between the Beige creed and the Nicene Creed?

For you, what's the main point(s) of the catechetical chef/cook analogy?

Make yourself some notes about the one or two things you take away most from this chapter.

PART 3

THE DIFFERENCE

HOLDING ENVIRONMENT

Perhaps the single most essential characteristic of *Teaching for Discipleship* is what doctors, educators, and leadership theorists call a "holding environment." This is a term first coined by the English pediatrician Donald Winnecott to describe the way a mother physically and emotionally cares for, or "holds," her child.

Psychologist and educator Robert Kegan later used it to describe the way a culture enables a person to find confirmation, contradiction, and continuity. Leadership expert Ronald Heifetz uses the notion of a holding environment to describe a workplace that enables people to tackle difficult problems and make adaptive changes.

But my affection for the concept of a "holding environment" comes from my wife Catherine's doctoral work on sustaining the Spirit fueling one's vocational calling. She has helped me borrow, baptize, and boil it down to this: *A holding environment is a sturdy and trustworthy place where people can do the difficult and intimate work of examining their beliefs, actions, attitudes, and values.*

Those engaged in *Teaching for Discipleship* first and foremost create and maintain a holding environment. Whether teaching third graders, facilitating a high school retreat, or conducting an

RCIA session, those engaged in T4D provide *a sturdy, trustworthy place where people can do the difficult and intimate work of examining their stuff.*

Within this formal or informal holding environment we create a sturdy, trustworthy place where young and old can do the intimate and often difficult work of examining perspectives, evaluating decisions, discovering blind spots, gaining knowledge, and praying.

This sturdy, trustworthy place must be able to handle the heat of disagreement, provide the comfort of mutual respect, supply honest conversation, and faithfully illuminate life experience with the light of Christ's teachings,

This is an intentional and foundational component of T4D.

The holding environment has everything to do with our quality of presence. It is something the catechist must dutifully establish and fiercely maintain. And it applies to faith formation that takes place in formal and informal settings.

This holding environment is maintained through a mixture of dynamics that are challenging and consoling, strategic and spontaneous, fast-paced and slowed down, prayerful and uncomfortable.

We will get to more specifics about these dynamics and the skills needed a bit later. For now, let us look at characteristics of T4D. When put together within a holding environment, they represent the difference between teaching for discipleship and some of our current approaches.

T4D assumes faith and points people to the More.

T4D remembers that people already believe and already come with the God-given ability to sense the sacred (see *Catechism*, 35). It starts with this assumption, expects it, and is not surprised when participants prove it.

On the other hand, T4D seeks to build on the faith of the community, shedding light on the More found in the life of discipleship.

> In learning to follow Christ, we become aware that there exist "facets of Christian life that come to full expression only by means of development and growth toward Christian maturity" (USCCB, *Called and Gifted for the Third Millennium*, 1995: 20). (NDC, 29)

> To put it more precisely: within the whole process of evangelization, the aim of catechesis is to be the teaching and maturation stage, that is to say, the period in which the Christian, having accepted by faith the person of Christ ... endeavors to know better this Jesus to whom he has entrusted himself: to know his "mystery," the Kingdom of God proclaimed by him, the requirements and promises contained in his Gospel message, and the paths that he has laid down for any one who wishes to follow him. (NDC, 19; see also *Catechesi Tradendae*, 20)

T4D strives to provide comprehensive formation.

> This comprehensive formation includes more than instruction: it is an apprenticeship of the entire Christian life, it is a "complete Christian initiation" (CT, 21), which promotes authentic following of Christ, focused on his Person; it implies education in knowledge of the faith and in the life of faith, in such a manner that the entire person, at his deepest levels, feels enriched by the word of God; it helps the disciple of Christ to transform the old man in order to assume his baptismal responsibilities and to profess the faith from the "heart." (GDC, 67)

T4D seeks to influence one's moral imagination.

Ask people what it means to be a good person and most will reply with some version of "don't be mean," "don't hurt anyone," "be respectful," etc. But T4D tries to expand a person's moral imagination, transforming one's self-image from the good self who does no harm to the proactive self who intentionally does good (see *Catechism*, 1803).

T4D also cultivates the moral imagination to serve something greater than oneself. By informally and formally exploring "the tradition of the calling," T4D tries to shape one's imagination of the expectation and the norms of discipleship: a lifelong formal and informal studying of the ways of the One and *actively applying* them.

T4D reclaims religious education.

Religious education has been given a bad rap. Over the last twenty-five years, we have associated religious education with instruction that lacked heart. We viewed it as education without inspiration, an academic approach that lacked soul, attending to the theological without investing in the relational.

Certainly, this kind of formation did exist, but it did not warrant the abandonment of religious education.

Real religious education blends information with discussion, prayer, and application. Religious education seeks to build religious literacy as well as religious experience. Religious education is intentional, systematic, and prayerful. When we turned our noses up at narrow examples of religious education and encouraged one another to move away from it, we lost the best aspects of it as well.

And what did we replace it with?

All kinds of stuff. Good stuff mostly. But we lost the principles of good education. We chose one method over another.

In my work with catechists over the past thirty years, I have noticed that one extreme or another can identify us. Either we preach on a topic, numb the group, and then throw out, "Any questions?" Or we share our own faith stories without employing effective ways to have those in attendance unpack their own. Or we do both these things without providing the aspect of our faith which illuminates our experience. Or we just decide to "meet people where they are" and let the issues of life determine the content of catechesis. Or we decide to focus on our favorite topic, Gospel teaching, Church doctrine, devotion, or spiritual interest, and forget to offer a more comprehensive formation.

Religious education employs principles of teaching and learning, education and formation that are too often overlooked today. Take, for example, something as basic as consciously incorporating techniques that are helpful to the visual learner, not just techniques suited for the auditory learner.

The Church reminds us:

Catechesis presents its service as a designated educative journey … [wherein] the catechist knows and avails of the contribution of the sciences of education, understood always in a Christian sense. (GDC, 147)

Both the Vatican and the U.S. bishops state clearly:

Perfect fidelity to Catholic doctrine is compatible with a rich diversity of presentation. (GDC, 122)

Religious education uses both inductive and deductive methods. In the *National Directory for Catechesis*, the bishops of the United States tell us:

Catechetical methods employ two fundamental processes that organize the human element in the communication of the faith: the *inductive method* and the *deductive method.* "The inductive approach proceeds from the sensible, visible, tangible experiences of the person, and leads, with the help of the Holy Spirit, to more general conclusions and principles" (National Catechetical Directory, 176).... The deductive method proceeds in the opposite manner, beginning with the general principles or truths of the faith and applying them to the concrete experiences of those to whom catechesis is addressed....

The deductive method corresponds to the "*kerygmatic*" approach ... [starting] with proclamation of the faith as it is expressed in the principal documents of the faith, such as Sacred Scripture, the Creeds, or the Liturgy, and applies it to human experiences.... The inductive method, on the other hand, corresponds to a more "existential" approach, beginning with the specifics of human experience and examining them in light of the Word of God.... Both are legitimate approaches when properly applied and are distinct yet complementary methods for communicating the faith. (29)

Inductive goes like this:
Life Experience   Aspect of the Faith   Response

Deductive goes like this:
Aspect of the Faith   Life Experience   Response

As a consultant for one Catholic publisher, I noticed that they framed the inductive method in three steps:

"What's the issue?" (experience)

"What's faith say?" (info)

"What now?" (response)

While the deductive approach would sound like this:

"Here's an aspect of the faith…"(info)

"Here's how it applies to life…" (experience)

"What aspect of your life is affirmed or challenged by
    this?" (response)

The Church is asking us to use both methods, and regardless of which method is used, the bishops tell us that a connection to experience must be made:

> Human experience is a constituent element in catechesis…. Human experiences provide the sensible signs that lead the person, by the grace of the Holy Spirit, to a better understanding of the truths of the faith. They are the means through which human beings come to know themselves, one another, and God….
>
> Catechesis helps them relate the Christian message to the most profound questions in life: the existence of God, the destiny of the human person, the origin and end of history, the truth about good and evil, the meaning of suffering and death, and so forth. (NDC, 29A)

The process of mediating this connection between faith to life and life to faith is what Pope Paul VI called the "drama of our time" (NDC, 29).

The Appendix in the back of this book provides examples to illustrate inductive and deductive methods.

Here is a summation gleaned from the Vatican's *General Directory for Catechesis*, the U.S. bishops' *National Directory for Catechesis* and the document *Renewing the Vision*. I compiled this from the actual wording within these documents without adding my own, and though it refers to catechesis among young people,

I submit that this summation applies to all catechists engaged in Teaching for Discipleship with any age group:

The catechist is essentially a mediator and a knowledgeable disciple, engaging adolescents through a variety of methods, activities, and learning approaches, including the use of media, music, memorization, group dynamics, liturgy, and prayer.

Helping young people read their experiences along with the questions and needs raised in light of the Gospel.

Offering them a spiritually challenging vision that helps young people meet their hunger to participate in the noble adventure of discipleship. (See GDC, 152-156; NDC, 48; RTV, p. 10)

T4D integrates meaningful experiences of prayer.
By incorporating aspects of the liturgy, sacramental symbols and signs, and naturally incorporating *deep* prayer experiences, T4D speaks to the soul in a different language. Providing participants with opportunities to experience prayers of thanksgiving, praise, worship, petition, contemplation, and even lamentation is a natural component in T4D. Inspired music can often move people more than our words, and T4D prays in all ways.

T4D evokes and examines (drives people out of their minds).
T4D avoids two extremes.
    One extreme common to faith formation resembles the selling or telling mode. This reflects a catechist's love for the spiri-

tual life and the heartfelt desire to share it with others in the hope of influencing their lives. It is common and understandable.

But the selling mode leaves only two responses, neither of which is desirable: a) people can "buy" what we are selling, maybe because they like us or see how important it is to us, without critically thinking about it or owning it; or b) they don't buy it.

The telling mode is limited because it is a one-way form of communicating, lacks any educational dynamics, and makes it easy for those in attendance to simply listen. Commonly referred to as "set and get," these one-way forms of presenting are formally referred to as "didactic" forms of teaching. We can dress these approaches up to be forms of "proclaiming the Good News" and "New Evangelization," but *Teaching for Discipleship* is different.

On the other extreme, we can overemphasize the value of "meeting people where they are" and "centering on their experiences" by asking people what they would like to discuss, what issues are on their minds, or what questions of faith they struggle with. This is also understandable and driven by a desire to be relevant and effective. But this kind of musing and wondering lacks direction and makes it impossible to systematically or intentionally take people to the More:

> Since adults are called to be disciples of Christ, the content of adult catechesis should be a catechesis directed toward discipleship. The content of such catechesis is *"cognitive, experiential, and behavioral."* (NDC, 48)

Instead of selling/telling or musing/wondering, *Teaching for Discipleship* centers on the process of evoking and examining.

	T4D	
selling	*evoking*	musing
telling	*examining*	wondering

Evoking and examining reflects the intentional discipline of formally and informally meeting people where they are ... *and driving them out of their minds* in order to consider the mind of Others ... the mind of Christ ... the mind of the Church.

HOLDING ENVIRONMENT TECHNIQUES

There are specific techniques that establish and maintain the holding environment, which is that *sturdy, trustworthy place where people can do the difficult and intimate work of examining their beliefs, actions, ambitions, attitudes, values.*

These techniques make T4D different than other approaches to faith formation, and it calls for certain skills.

While my wife and I were working on our doctorates, we picked up a book written by a colleague, Sharon Daloz Parks, entitled *Leadership Can Be Taught.* Dr. Parks has a theological background and for many years focused on the spiritual formation of young adults before moving into leadership education. The title of her book stands in bold contrast to the many leadership theories which insist that leadership is something you are either born with or not. Her book details the way Ronald Heifetz, mentioned earlier in this chapter, teaches aspiring leaders attending his classes at Harvard's Kennedy School of Government.

A wonderful thing happened as soon as I began to read it: by Page 4, where she addresses the question "Can Leadership Be Taught?" I felt compelled to change the word leadership to *discipleship.* It was not something I planned on doing. I believe it was providential.

That single book pushed me to sift and sort and weigh the similar ways that *discipleship* can be taught. I underlined, folded the corners of pages, and scribbled notes throughout. And based on my own life's work as a religious educator, I found the following dynamics apply to *Teaching for Discipleship*. They are detailed here not in a prescriptive manner — if you do this then all will be well. Nor do you have to practice all of them in order to engage in *Teaching for Discipleship*. But together they present the picture, the profile, the nature of a certain and deliberate way of teaching.

Naming the Challenge

T4D clearly identifies the challenge or opportunity "on the table" for examination during a particular session. Regardless of the setting or the related discussions that may carry the group up around the moon and back again (in a good way), those engaged in *Teaching for Discipleship* consistently remind the group of the topic — the IT at hand — be it a moral dilemma, a teaching of Christ, a doctrine of the Church, a spiritual practice, or the theme of a prayer experience. And usually the IT being examined during a session may invite a change in attitude, belief, or behavior.

This may sound obvious to some, but too often, those leading a session or an experience allow its main topic/challenge/opportunity to be blurred and buried. Naming and reminding participants of the IT meant to be examined in the session provides clarity, maintains the purpose of the session, and often makes it more difficult for participants to avoid coming to terms with the challenge that the IT may pose to them personally.

Regulating the Heat

The holding environment is a sturdy, trustworthy place that can handle the heat of disagreement, emotions, and frustration that come whenever people do the difficult and intimate work of examination.

Those engaged in *Teaching for Discipleship* intentionally regulate that heat much like a cook regulates a cooktop. One has to know when to turn up the heat in order to have things cooking and when to turn down the heat so that no one gets hurt or the topic gets burned to toast.

Sometimes, to turn up the heat, those who are *Teaching for Discipleship* will articulate an opposing point of view, even if it is not their own, just to further evoke and examine — that is, "Some people say .... because they think that .... What do you say/think about that?"

Sometimes, to turn down the heat, it is best to summarize the point of the discussion and move forward.

Protecting All the Voices

In order for one's presence to be a sturdy, trustworthy place, one has to ensure that every participant can contribute without being marginalized, minimized, or categorized. In working with teens, for example, this means respecting the input of that young person who — in a moment of illumination and authenticity — makes a noble statement about the merits and courage of a virtuous act even though everyone else in the room knows that this young person is living a life quite contrary to the insight he or she just shared.

It also means ensuring that the adult RCIA candidate who is grinding an axe due to his or her own agenda is once again allowed to share it without others in the room discrediting that person's input.

Protecting all the voices *does not mean tacitly approving* of everyone's perspective. Nor does it mean accommodating moral relativism. It means fiercely and faithfully maintaining an environment that allows everyone to feel safe doing the difficult and intimate work of examination.

Rules of Engagement

My all-time favorite urban educator, Dr. Lorraine Monroe, was known for her work turning around educational practices among

New York City's children. She showed everyone how to raise expectations and lower tolerances. She fiercely amped up the way her school(s) demanded certain things from its students and its teachers. One of the things she was fond of saying was: "You can't teach in chaos. I don't care who you are … Jesus, Moses, Gandhi … You cannot teach in chaos!"

But too often, we do. Good-hearted as we are, we sometimes allow too much chaos to exist in our presence.

In order to maintain *a sturdy, trustworthy place wherein people can do the difficult and intimate work of examination,* T4D posts and enforces a few rules of engagement. A few rules are necessary to maintain a holding environment, and there are many helpful versions out there. Rules of engagement are essential in T4D.

Once you have the ones you want there are two things that must be done:

1. Post them for all to see.

2. Refer back to them whenever one or more is violated.

It doesn't matter whether it's a third-grade religion class, a sophomore retreat, vacation Bible school, or an RCIA session. Post and refer back when needed.

I have my own four rules of engagement when *Teaching for Discipleship*:

- Say Anything (appropriately)

- One at a Time

- No Put-downs

- Participate, Participate, Participate

Using Powerful Questions

Avoid three kinds of questions: Mickey Mouse ones, manipulative ones, and Yes/No ones.

Mickey Mouse questions are those that are superficial, sweet, or safe. They are a waste of time, they dumb down the experience, and they bore people.

Manipulative questions are the ones we use to drag people to our perspective. Usually, they are questions that only have one obvious answer. We pose them because we know that the correct answer moves people away from their perspective and over to "our side." We follow one of these questions with one or two more so that the obvious — and often the oversimplistic answers — lead people over to "our side." People know when we are manipulating them with these kinds of questions. When we use this kind of question we lose respect and trust. In a workshop recently, a teacher said that this is exactly the technique used when someone knocked on her door with a religious pamphlet.

Yes/No questions offer an easy exit for those who do not wish to engage or examine. They can simply hit the No button and opt out — that is, "Have you ever … ?" "No." Or they say "Yes" but don't/can't give a reason. Rephrasing the question to something like "When was the last time you…?" increases the chances that people can respond by sharing a piece of their experience. It also reflects one of the basic principles of T4D: people already have some spiritual experiences/insights. Expect it.

Several years ago, I was leading a youth session and the IT on the table was discernment and "listening to the Spirit." Fifteen of us sat in a circle. I was a guest and did not know any of these kids.

For twenty minutes, we discussed what makes it hard to discern the voice of the Spirit, what can distract us from hearing the voice of the Spirit, etc. It was an okay discussion, and we were able to identify a few things.

Finally, I asked them a question I had never used before. Since we were not talking about doctrine and there was no correct theological answer or fact, I asked, "What have you *found to be true* about the way the Spirit talks to you?" They all looked at me. So I slowly asked it again. Two more times. Then the kids brought it. For ten minutes they brought their answers and gave examples. One would respond and three others would nod in agreement.

At one point, the adult sitting next to me whispered under his breath, "My goodness." I have used this question regularly ever since, as long as the IT on the table is not related to doctrine or religious literacy.

What is it about this question?

Questions like this work because they are open-ended and *assume people have the experience to respond.* These types of questions have more potential and are more powerful ways to help people do the difficult and intimate work of examination. I am not good at this. I often have to restate a question like this several times in order to find the best way to word it for the group I am working with.

T4D uses powerful questions instead of the Mickey Mouse, manipulative, or Yes/No ones because they take everyone deeper sooner.

Holding Steady

In the midst of engaging people in the difficult and intimate work of examination, T4D does not abdicate what it believes to be true, noble, wise, right. Somewhere along the way, we mistakenly thought that faith formation meant holding everyone's views to be valid because of each person's own personal truth.

Holding steady in the face of rejection and disagreement means being able to remain clear about the teaching of Christ, the wisdom of a moral principle, or an aspect of the Tradition in the midst of evoking and examining. This is different than giving everyone's perspective the same weight as the Gospel.

Holding steady while maintaining the sturdy, trustworthy place is a combination of affirmation and resistance. To do this requires that each of us find our own voice. More specifically, the right *ministerial tone of voice*.

Years ago, I was facilitating the Teaching for Spiritual Growth at the Weston Jesuit School of Theology. The group consisted of twenty Catholic inner-city teachers and youth ministers. Dr. Robert Coles had led them in a discussion of a short story and somehow the topic of finding your ministerial tone of voice came up. One participant said: "Finding the right tone of my voice is hard! Sometimes I feel like a bull in a china closet, and sometimes I feel like the china in a bull's closet."

In the right voice, we faithfully maintain the teachings of the One and the wisdom of Christian morality with soft eyes and a truthful tongue. In the right voice, people hear our conviction without hearing animosity. Holding steady with the right ministerial tone of voice requires what Sharon Parks calls "a strong tenderness and a tender strength."

Appreciating Failure

Corporations spend millions trying to learn from failure. *Teaching for Discipleship* regularly places failure front and center as a way to evoke examination:

> "Tell of a time when you were given good advice, but you ignored it and it was a big mistake." "Tell of a time when you gave someone advice, and they followed it, but it was disastrous."

> "Tell of a time when you wanted to tell the truth but you didn't and now you regret it." "Tell of a time when

you told the truth but you wish you would have found another way to say it."

"I made a decision once that I am still feeling bad about…."

"So this athlete decides to go to the party after the game. At the party … and now this person has been dismissed from the team and lost the scholarship."

Teaching for Discipleship uses examples of failure as a teaching tool and as a reminder of our imperfection. And just as importantly, T4D often uses failure with a blend of humor and humility. Failure, again, in the right ministerial tone of voice, acknowledges the struggle and folly found in our attempts to walk the right way and encourages people to be reflective learners. Appreciating failure in an honest, authentic, geez-what-was-I-thinking way reinforces the sturdy, trustworthy nature of our presence.

Written Reflection

Teaching for Discipleship incorporates structured *written* reflection. Too often we skip this dynamic. We prefer verbal exchanges. T4D builds in written reflection *before or after* verbal expression and intentionally builds the capacity for written reflection as a lifelong practice.

Written reflection is a disciplined practice that forces one to put whatever is in one's head or heart *on paper*, where one can see it with one's own eyes and perhaps hear oneself say it. This practice of written reflection captures and brings to visible form valuable thoughts or sentiments that have no form or expression.

T4D integrates disciplined written reflection with all age groups and can be accompanied by music or conducted in a prayerful space. It can be offered through "free write" exercises or more formal worksheets, journal exercises, etc.

Speech pathologists refer to a "cognitive-linguistic gap" between a thought one has in one's head and the ability it takes to verbalize it. Ever notice how some children and youths grimace and make faces as they try to articulate a thought, verbally answer a question, or share what's in their heart? Some have a larger cognitive-linguistic gap than others. This gap closes the older we get. But it is another reason why written reflection makes things easier for everyone.

Watching the Pace

Much like regulating the heat, watching the pace is a facilitation task that calls for observation and adjustment. Those engaged in *Teaching for Discipleship* are fully present to the moment while also *observing* the moment to see if things are moving too fast or too slow.

While one or two participants might be fully engaged in an exercise or discussion, the veteran catechist, like any trained educator, must be able to recognize if the rest of the group is ready to move on. Sometimes it is best to impose shorter time spans for the completion of exercises as a way of adding a sense of urgency to the tasks and picking up the pace. Other times it may be best to slow things down so that a deeper level of examination or reflection can take place.

The point is, *Teaching for Discipleship* includes paying close attention to pace and making the necessary adjustments in the midst of the session.

Good Sonar

This is the ability to hear what is beneath the surface: the question behind the question, the statement found behind one's eyes, the nonverbals in one's body language, etc. With good sonar we are attuned to some things that are below the surface of something said. Good sonar gives us the ability to see, hear, or recognize what may be hidden below, or inside.

I was teaching a class on communication in the Master of Ministry program at Creighton University one semester. I brought this idea to the group, and we discussed it. Good sonar, we all agreed, is a valuable asset to ministry — and I would add *Teaching for Discipleship*.

Just as we were about to move on to another topic, a man asked to offer one more thought about good sonar. He explained that he was retired Navy, and that he had a lot of actual experience with sonar at sea. What he shared with us next says so much about those who want to maintain the holding environment, which is at the core of T4D.

"You know what makes for good sonar?" he asked me.

"No, I don't."

"You think of sonar and you think of the ability to pick up signals coming from something underneath the surface and all, right?"

"Right."

"But the secret to good sonar, the secret to picking up a good signal, is the quality of the signal you send out." And with that he waved his hand slowly forward from his chest toward the rest of us. "It depends on the quality of the signal you send out." He repeated with his hand extending from his chest to mine.

I have often referred back to this paradox.

Our ability to send out signals of empathy, respect, and understanding somehow brings peoples' unspoken responses closer to the surface so that we might glimpse them.

Affirmation/Resistance

Teaching for Discipleship welcomes and affirms all that comes with people doing the difficult and intimate work of examination.

Doing so helps make your presence a trustworthy place.

And T4D also pushes back and challenges people in order to drive them out of their minds and into the mind of others, the mind of Christ, and the mind of the Church.

Sometimes resistance to a stated point of view or moral perspective is needed in order to help your presence also be a place where people can do the difficult and intimate work of examination. In T4D, adding this kind of stress is intentional. It evokes examination.

Mediating this process of connecting faith to life and life to faith requires both affirmation and resistance. Too much of either one can weaken what can be sturdy and jeopardize that which might be trustworthy.

It requires a sense of the Spirit and the Wisdom of the Ratio (which we'll learn about in Part 4).

"Go-To Stories"

I got this from John Shea, a theologian and an iconic Catholic storyteller. We have worked on some stories together, and I have learned more about the spiritual life from him than I have from any other one person. He has spent the last several years helping the next generation of lay leaders assume positions of responsibility within Catholic health care. The nuns and religious communities that own these hospitals want the new generation of lay leaders to understand the mission, values, and charism of their healing institutions.

Several years ago, he was describing the curriculum he has formed for these hospital leaders and at one point referred to the necessity of always having a couple of stories on hand in case he needed them to illustrate a point he was making or to reinforce a point being made by one of the participants. He called these stories "Go-To Stories" and cheerfully compared them to a core collection of plays a coach offers the team when it mattered most.

A "go-to play" is one that has a history of being effective and you can go to it when you just have to have a moment of success.

So it is with *Teaching for Discipleship*. We need a small, core collection of stories that we can "go to" to help evoke examination, shed fresh light on a blessed truth or a moral principle, and/or prod some small measure of awakening.

Nothing serves these functions like good narrative, be it an Old Testament saga, a contemporary song, a poem, a parable, or a short story. Narrative, in its various forms, is a welcomed and trusted resource in *Teaching for Discipleship*.

Using Silence

During the summer of my third year teaching in a Catholic school, while in my twenties, I decided to get my real estate license. The young broker who sold Cathy and me our first little, one-thousand-square-foot house assured me that the extra money I could make in the summer would allow me to keep teaching.

The first thing he did was to make me watch videotapes led by the legendary salesman Zig Ziglar. I didn't know or care who Zig Ziglar was. I just wanted to get my license and hunt for a sale.

But one thing Zig Ziglar preached was the proper use of silence. Specifically, he would point out that silence was crucial after you asked the right question. He insisted that the most important thing to do after asking the critically important closing question — that is, "So, Mr. and Mrs. Smith, will this house work for you?" was to shut the heck up. He would scream into the camera, "SHUT UP!!!!!"

This is also true in *Teaching for Discipleship*. We have already mentioned the use of powerful questions. These questions are hard to find and invaluable tools when you do find them. But too often we ask a powerful question and, after a few seconds of no response, we break the silence and once again give participants an escape hatch from which they can avoid the difficult and intimate work of examination. Ziglar's point was that silence forces someone to deal with the question.

Ever since those early days in my career, I have developed the practice of asking a decent question and refusing to break the silence. Count the cracks in the tile; gently repeat the question; think about what you are going to eat afterward; repeat the question again; maybe look around the room; but sit still and wait. Do not break the silence. Let silence do the heavy lifting.

Susan Scott, in her *New York Times* bestseller *Fierce Conversations* points out that silence forces one to wrestle with the question. Silence helps bring forward the person's response from within. She also reminds us that some insights and emotions need silence in order to find their rightful place on the table. In fact, the more emotion behind a response, the more silence it deserves.

Those engaged in *Teaching for Discipleship* can use silence to slow down the pace after an emotional response. Others can use silence to evoke the disciplined written reflection mentioned earlier. Like white space on a page of type, silence helps us take things in, better understand, and feel. This is an important dynamic in *Teaching for Discipleship*.

Too often, those of us who facilitate faith formation do not know the place and merits of silence. In *Fierce Conversations*, Scott shares a famous Native American question: "*Where in your life did you become uncomfortable with the sweet territory of silence?*"

Aiming at Awakenings

All of us engaged in the ministry of catechesis pray that our efforts help open those we serve to the experience of conversion. Through the grace of God, our hearts hold dear the possibility that those we teach, lead, serve will make small and big changes — away from harmful ways and toward loving ways, away from vices and toward virtues, away from secular goals and toward spiritual ones.

Conversion, after all, is about making a change. And God knows we all need to make changes.

The *Catechism of the Catholic Church* reminds us that there are two kinds of conversions: initial and ongoing.

Initial conversion in gained through baptism. Ongoing conversion is something made possible through the grace of God.

The *Catechism* says ongoing conversion is a "movement of a 'contrite heart'" (1428), "a radical reorientation" (1431), "a return" (1431), and "an end of sin, a turning away from evil" (1431). But there is danger in overemphasizing conversion. When, and if, we become preoccupied with conversion, we actually place it further out of reach.

There is a difference between conversion and awakening. Our tradition and most spiritual traditions understand awakening to consist of a new way of understanding, a new insight, an illumination, an "aha." Conversion is a change in attitude, behavior, values, ambitions, made after we have an awakening.

Awakenings help a person see differently and then perhaps act or think differently. The tradition has always been that awakenings, these new insights, lead a person, with the grace of God, to make a change. Awakenings lead to conversion.

God knows we all need conversion. But a preoccupation with conversion can actually make it more difficult.

Danger number one: A preoccupation with conversion can cause us to ignore aiming at awakenings. In sports terms, we swing for the home run of conversion and miss the chance to get the base hits of awakenings. We pursue the seventy-yard touchdown pass and not the first down. We structure our efforts toward the game winning three-pointer and ignore the layup. We aim for the extraordinary at the expense of the ordinary. And when we don't get it we tend to blame the participants and speak of their unbelief, lack of readiness, spiritual apathy, or their parents.

Our books, our documents, and our conventions are full of references to the need for conversions. But there is little mention of the role of awakenings.

When was the last time you had a professional conversation about aiming at awakenings? And how might aiming at awakenings help facilitate conversion?

Danger number two: Focusing too much on conversion instead of awakenings shapes the quality of our presence and our ministerial tone of voice. For example, a person who needs awakening must be in what state? *Asleep.* A person in need of conversion must be in what state? There are several answers we can choose from such as, "on the wrong path," "in a state of sin," "on a path of evil," "lost," "needing redirection."

Awakening implies that people we teach are *asleep*. When we think the people we teach are in need of conversion, we send the signal that they are in a state more egregious, harmful, or negative than asleep. It shapes our ministerial tone of voice. It shapes the quality of our presence. And they can smell it on us, putting the possibility of conversion further away.

T4D aims at awakenings, calling all to awaken from the spiritual sleep induced by the lullabies of the postmodern culture.

T4D trusts the ability of the Spirit to prod awakenings as mentioned in the *Catechism* (see 683-687, 732).

T4D monitors the degree to which our desire for conversion impacts the way we lead beige believers to the More.

In Summary

Teaching for Discipleship is about formally and informally exploring the "tradition of the calling." People already believe. T4D is what comes after the seeds sown have taken root. This root word for disciple is student. A disciple studies the ways of the One and lives by them.

T4D is about meeting people where they are in order to *drive them out of their minds* … and into the mind of others … into the mind of Christ … into the mind of the Church.

T4D seeks to pitch a tent in one's moral imagination: transforming one's self-image from the good person who does no harm to the proactive person who intentionally does good (see *Catechism*, 1803). It also cultivates the moral imagination, which can fuel the commitment to serve something greater than oneself.

Within the formal or informal "holding environment," we create a sturdy, trustworthy place where young and old can do the intimate and often difficult work of examining perspectives, evaluating decisions, discovering blind spots, gaining knowledge, and praying.

This sturdy, trustworthy place must be able to handle the heat of disagreement, provide the comfort of mutual respect, supply honest conversation, and faithfully illuminate life experience with the light of Christ's teachings, in order to engage people in the "drama of our time."

Using both inductive and deductive methods, T4D names the challenges, focuses on the issues, protects all the voices in the house, regulates the heat, watches the pace, uses questions that go deeper sooner, incorporates disciplined reflection, and is not afraid of the proper use of repetition or memorization.

T4D offers authentic affirmation while holding steady in the face of resistance. It embraces experiences of failure that shed light on a better way to live, employs good sonar by hearing what is underneath, intentionally uses silence, and makes words count.

But *more than anything else,* T4D is a way of *being with* people and uses listening as the central dynamic, for without active and deep listening, you won't know what to do or when to do it.

For Reflection

If someone asked you to sum up the difference between *Teaching for Discipleship* and other approaches, what would you say?

Which method do you tend to use the most, inductive or deductive? What percentage of the time do you use it?

To what degree has your catechetical approach served as a holding environment? What can you do to keep it that way, or move it toward being *a sturdy, trustworthy place where people can do the difficult and intimate work of examining their beliefs, actions, attitudes, and values?*

For Reflection

T4D techniques include:

Naming the Challenge

Regulating the Heat

Protecting All the Voices

Rules of Engagement

Using Powerful Questions

Holding Steady

Appreciating Failure

Written Reflection

Watching the Pace

Good Sonar

Affirmation/Resistance

"Go-To Stories"

Using Silence

Aiming at Awakenings

Place a check mark by the one(s) you currently employ in your teaching. Place a * by the one(s) that you know you have used in the past but haven't employed recently. Circle the one(s) that you would like to make a more active part of your teaching.

PART 4

TEACHING INFORMALLY
AND KEEPING HEART

From the beginning, discipleship not only implied study, it has also implied apprenticeship. So far we have examined *Teaching for Discipleship* in a formal, structured way, but the informal teaching common to mentoring or accompanying can also play an important role.

3-D SPIRITUALITY

But before describing five ways we can accompany or mentor someone on the path of discipleship, let's look at the different dimensions of spirituality. Each of these three dimensions has a primary "direction," and that direction often reflects the dominant focus of our spirituality.

Some of us have a strong "vertical" spirituality that focuses primarily on our relationship with the transcendent God "above." Those of us with a highly vertical spirituality invest in our prayer lives, think a lot about the "things of God," ask questions about the nature of God, strive to maintain and enhance our personal relationship with God, and are willing to make time for worship.

Those with a dominant vertical dimension to their spirituality will often say things like: "God and I are close." "I couldn't make it through the day without my prayer time." "I think about God a lot, and I ask my religion teachers a lot of God questions."

Some of us have a strong "horizontal" spirituality wherein we place an emphasis on treating others with compassion, charity, kindness, and love. Those of us with a highly horizontal dimension seem interested in justice, service, fairness, equality, and moral living.

Those with a strong horizontal dimension to their spirituality express interest in service projects, will raise questions about current events, and have a keen sensitivity for fairness. We might be heard to say things like: "Because of my faith, I try to accept everyone no matter the race or religion." "My word is good. I don't go online and rip people with rumors." "I try to pay attention to the kids in school who get left out of things."

Those of us with a dominant "internal" dimension to our spirituality focus on the power of faith to bring a sense of inner peace, a sense of hope, and the ability to cope with the things that hurt inside. While psychologists might refer to these folks as having emotional intelligence and resiliency, spiritually speaking, these are folks whose faith helps them bounce back from disappointment, heal over past hurts, and generally navigate the roller coaster of life with a soulful sense of comfort.

These are folks who will say things like: "Because of my faith, I'm better able to handle my anger." "My faith is the main reason I'm not as sad as I used to be." "Because of my faith, I'm accepting myself more, even with my imperfections." "Because of my faith, I'm better able to just let go and move on."

In the extreme, we can invest so much in the dominant dimension of our spirituality that we prevent it from influencing the other dimensions of the spiritual life. For example, those with a highly vertical dimension can create a spirituality that truly invests in a prayerful relationship with God but doesn't carry over into the way they treat others (horizontal): I can pray regularly and still tell racist jokes or cheat on my taxes. Teens can pray for the soldiers at war and grandma's health and still sleep around.

Those of us with an extremely horizontal spirituality may find ourselves neglecting the vertical dimension and saying something like: "I believe in God and all. And I know God is watching over me and stuff, but I don't pray much, and I don't see why you have to go to church. What God really wants is for me to be a loving person."

And those of us with an extremely internal dimension can enjoy spiritual strength, inner peace, and happiness, and yet not feel propelled to worship (vertical) or compelled to serve others (horizontal).

I don't believe that one age group or gender has a dominant dimension more so than another. But I do believe that we each may undergo different spiritual seasons when our spiritual interests and energy seem naturally drawn to one dimension and then to another.

These three dimensions are distinct and yet overlap. Each has its primary direction but naturally spills over to the other dimensions. These three dimensions are akin to faith, hope, and love. Faith is usually associated with a vertical belief and trust in the One. Hope usually refers to an internal asset. And love usually refers to a horizontal dynamic. But we can also have faith in one another, in oneself. And our hope can be born from faith. And love can be directed to the transcendent as well as others.

All this relates to, formally or informally, *Teaching for Discipleship*:

1. T4D intentionally tries to cultivate all three dimensions in those we serve. T4D constantly asks: "How and when is our work cultivating the vertical? How and when are

we cultivating the horizontal? How and when are we cultivating the internal dimension of spirituality?"

2. Those engaged in T4D deliberately try to glimpse the dominant dimension(s) in those we teach, affirm it, and invite participants to cultivate their less developed dimension.

3. We can unconsciously evaluate the spirituality of those we teach by how much their dominant spiritual dimension correlates to our own favorite dimension. Those of us with a dominant vertical dimension will bemoan the group that "won't settle into prayer experiences," or "refuses to see the value of Sunday Mass." Those of us with a dominant horizontal dimension bemoan those who "don't care about anyone outside their own group," or "couldn't care less about the poor," or "are so rude to each other." And those of us with a dominant internal dimension bemoan those who "get crushed over every little thing," or "are so concerned about [fill in the blank] instead of just trusting the Lord."

4. T4D requires us to personally identify our own dominant dimension and set aside a season to cultivate a less developed dimension.

5. Because of these three different dimensions, there is more opportunity for faith-filled adults to participate in the spiritual formation of others. For example, the coach who helps a player to find the spiritual strength to deal with anger or failure is now a teacher helping cultivate the internal dimension of the spiritual life. The aunt, uncle, or school counselor helping a teen find the appropriate

moral way to express affection is now a teacher cultivating the horizontal dimension of the spiritual life.

These three dimensions open the door for the contributions that can be made by those who do not have the knowledge, skill, or comfort level needed to cultivate the vertical dimension.

Teaching Informally

My doctoral work years ago, and the experience I have had since then, has helped me recognize at least five informal ways any faith-filled adult can participate in the spiritual journey of children and youths regardless of their relationship, role, education, training, or background. These five informal dynamics are not the same as the formal dynamics we have been looking at up to this point. They make up the dynamics of accompanying or mentoring. And instead of using helpful textbooks, these informal ways of teaching use the con*text* of people's lives. Perhaps you can find one or two that is most compatible to your personality and your own natural set of gifts and skills.

Attending to Stories

This activity is not to be confused with "telling stories," or "teaching with stories." In fact, it is just the opposite. This is about paying attention to the stories children and youths are reading, watching on television, paying for at the cinema, discussing among themselves after school, or listening to on their headphones.

The key task to this activity is to attend to the story, pull out the theme, and use that theme as a bridge to a soulful conversation. It requires that you pay attention to the stories being discussed — often in the back seat of the car on the way back from a ballgame.

Asking a simple question often can identify a theme: "So, what was that movie/story/song/show about?" or "What's the issue with that whole situation?" If the response is anything like Forgiveness or Letting Go, you can walk it along with, "Don't know about you, but that's so hard for me to do," or "Nice. I just let go of something recently. Took me awhile. Not as good at it as I should be. You?"

Certain story themes evoke spiritual issues:

Confession Loss Vulnerability Labeling Blindness Hope Power Fear Evil Redemption Awakenings Aspirations Pain Fierce Determination The Sacred Resiliency Hypocrisy The System Anger Failure Self-doubt Death Afterlife Angels Unaware Discipleship The Moral Life Searching

Simply put, the task in Attending to Stories is to pull out the theme and use it as a bridge to the vertical, horizontal, or internal dimension of the spiritual life.

Building Skills

This dynamic involves intentionally teaching specific ways to improve the Religious (vertical), Moral (horizontal), Emotional (internal) dimensions of spirituality. It requires a coaching style of instruction — for example, how to pray with the Bible, how to keep the Sabbath, how to get and give second chances, how to recognize God's presence, how to stay hopeful when a bad thing happens. Often this can include introducing people to spiritual practices such as contemplation — the one Jesus pointed to in the story of Martha and Mary (see Lk 10:38-42).

Methods vary when it comes to Building Skills for spiritual growth. Some skills are best built through direct instruction, such as the one Jesus gave regarding almsgiving (see Mt 6:1-4). Some skills are built by offering practice opportunities for skills one may have let go dormant — for example, examining your conscience.

The key to building some skills can often be generated by the individuals we are working with, especially skills that are integral to their everyday lives. They are often closer to the challenge than we are and have more experience with the challenge than we have. This is the approach I take when helping teens build the spiritual skill of expressing affection. I give them a few hypothetical situations and have them come up with the concrete steps or principles.

Like this: *A classmate of the opposite sex has been tutoring you so you can improve your SAT math scores. After a few months of tutoring, you take the test, get a better score and now want to express the affection you have for this person. Now come up with two appropriate ways, one inappropriate way, and a couple of things to keep in mind when it comes to expressing affection.*

Helping others increase their vocabulary can also be a helpful technique in building a skill. Vocabulary empowers people to better describe an experience, a goal, or a constructive vertical, horizontal, or internal action.

Honoring the Senses

When it comes to sensing the sacred, children and youths tend to use two ingredients more than adults do: *Emotionality* and *Imagination*.

When we adults have "God moments," for example, we tend to make a mental connection along the lines of, "So this is what they were talking about when ..." or "Now I understand what he/she/that means." Our God moments may be emotional ones, but we tend to go to the cognitive with it rather quickly.

Children and youths stay on a more affective level when they sense the sacred. I always ask young people when in the last six months they have felt closest to God. One individual told me he felt so close to God at a recent rock concert: "It was awesome! We were in the front row. Standing room only, totally sold out concert, and we were in the front row!"

He repeated it a couple of time. I finally said: "I get it. I get it. Front row." He went on: "No man you don't get it. We were in the *front row* of this awesome concert. Me and my friends had been singing and swaying and sweating and everyone was cheering, and I looked down the row at my friends, and I was so grateful to be at this awesome concert. And it was just the warm-up band! The real band hadn't even come out yet! So I just thanked God for letting me get to go to this awesome concert with my friends. But then I started thanking God for all kinds of things. Different things came to my head that I hadn't thought about in a long time. I thanked God for, like, everything."

This young man had a mini-mystical experience of gratitude in the front row of a concert.

Now some of us might want to follow up by asking him if he smelled what was in the third row, or if he listened to the lyrics, in the hope of pointing out a moral this or that. But that wasn't the question I had asked him. I had asked him when he had felt closest to God in the last six months.

Honoring the Senses is all about respecting the way children and youths sense the sacred affectively much more than they do cognitively.

Children and youths use Emotionality and Imagination (E/I) to make sense of five kinds of spiritual moments:

1. "aha" moments of discovery
2. moments of religious and/or moral confrontation
3. spiritually historical or eventful occasions
4. moments of grace and strength
5. moments related to place(s)

And often the use of E/I leads to the enshrinement of possessions associated with a particular spiritual moment.

I videotaped a number of interviews once around the topic of "What's your favorite Catholic season or symbol?"

One young person said, "The Tridiuum is my favorite season, because these are the three key days that make up Holy Week." And she proceeded to explain each of the three days to me. Then she said that her favorite symbol was the *ichthys* and explained how the first Christians used this fish symbol as a secret sign of their belief during persecutions in the early years of the Church. It was apparent that a big reason she loved this season and symbol is because she *understood* it cognitively.

When I show the video of the various interviews, many adults mention how her remarks stood out from the rest of the teens interviewed. That's because she is like us. She had gained the theological/liturgical/historical knowledge of it, and it brought her joy. She had decoded Holy Week and the ancient yet contemporary symbol of the *ichthys*. And because she had decoded it, learned the meaning of it, she *loved* it.

She stood out from the others because she had an adult appreciation when compared to the rest of the teens who said things like: "Christmas, because it's the warmest time of the year." "All Souls' Day, because I've had a lot of friends who have died." "The dove is my favorite symbol because it stands for peace."

The best example of how children and youths use emotion and imagination in making sense of the sacred came from another young person in the same group as the young lady above.

When asked the same question, "What's your favorite Catholic season or symbol?" this teen responded before the videographer could refocus his camera and before the guy with the boom mic could reach over to the middle of the group. I knew it at the time, but I didn't want to ask that young person to repeat it for the camera. It went unrecorded, but I try to make sure it does not go untold.

"Incense is my favorite symbol," the teen said. I knew what was coming next. Something about how the way the smoke rises up like our prayers rise up to the heavens. But then I told myself to wait, there will be a twist, perhaps something about how smoke fills the room to show us how "God is in the house." Yeah, that's what's coming next I told myself. Smoke rising up, like our prayers, or smoke filling the place like God's presence among us.

Then the young person brought it. Please notice the role Emotionality and Imagination plays in making sense of the sacred:

"Incense is my favorite because it reminds me that you always pray best after you get burned."

Offering Solidarity

This is different than "standing in solidarity" with those we teach, lead, or serve. Sometimes standing in solidarity with someone only brings that person more attention than she or he wants. Sometimes it brings that person more embarrassment than he or she is already struggling with.

Offering Solidarity signals your willingness to accompany, support, or stand with another *if* it is desired. It is done in a way that sends the signal he or she can decline your offer without any difficulty or question. A parishioner struggling with the actions of his or her child in college, or a spousal issue, may not want you to stand in solidarity, but might appreciate you offering it.

We were discussing this in a graduate course I was teaching at St. John's College in Collegeville, Minnesota. A high school teacher immediately responds: "I'm there. We had a student die a week ago. I go to the wake. Walk into the funeral home that night and see three of my students huddled together crying. I take a step toward them, but they turned their back on me, so I went straight to the body and knelt by the casket."

Another teacher replies: "I just don't get it. The kids were crying and you just walked away. How's this a good thing?"

The first one responded: "They knew I was willing to be with them. But when they turned their back on me I knew it was too much for them. For whatever reason, they weren't ready or open or wanting me to get involved."

I asked, "Did they really turn their backs on you?" The response: "Oh, no. Just a slight turn of their shoulders. It was all I needed to see."

Those students knew that their teacher was Offering Solidarity. And that teacher was awake enough to see the offer being declined and open enough to accept the decline. To have "stood in solidarity" with those students in that situation would have put more weight on shoulders already burdened.

Attending to Stories requires a cognitive task: find the spiritual theme in the story and use it as a bridge to a soulful conversation.

Building Skills has a behavioral focus, teaching someone how to attend to a vertical, horizontal, or internal task.

Honoring the Senses calls for respecting the affective ways people sense the sacred.

Offering Solidarity is a relational dynamic applied to at least nine different situations calling for: *Moral Courage   Advocacy   Achievement   Religious Experience   Pain   The Search for Truth   Spiritual Direction   School   Passions*

Offering Solidarity is not something all of us can do well, because not all of us have the innate relational ability to demonstrate what it requires: *Humility   Questioning   Quality of Presence   Authenticity   Comfort with Contradictions   Personal Support   Resourcefulness   Dissatisfaction   Reverence for Family   Strength of Spirit*

Cultivating Spiritual Sensitivity

This dynamic requires that we use the context of one's life as a textbook to help one develop "ears to hear, eyes to see" the spiritual wisdom or insight being offered to that person at that time.

Through this dynamic, we *prod awakenings* based on whatever that person is dealing with, wondering about, trying to make sense of, etc.

Cultivating Spiritual Sensitivity comes from reminding someone:

- Spiritual growth involves *thinking* and *doing*.

- Spiritual sensitivity involves seeing past the physical and the social. It requires discipline.

- There are tests from time to time to see how well you are developing.

- You move within a communion of saints, so keep an open mind.

- Spiritual Sensitivity involves the authentic pursuit of truth, including core truth about yourself.

- Keeping Sabbath is critical for sustaining spiritual sensitivities.

- You need reminders: slogans, objects, songs, places, memories, rituals, traditions, stories.

- "Spirit illuminates the mind, gladdens the heart, activates the will."

The last quote above is something else my wife and I were taught by John Shea, who also points out that most of the time the Spirit brings all three. He said that if you have an illumination, but it does not activate your will, then you are not being inspired. Likewise, if your will is activated, but your mind is not illuminated, then you are not inspired.

Cultivating Spiritual Sensitivity is a dynamic best pursued by adults who have already developed this sensitivity themselves but don't tend to shine their light in other people's eyes. It requires that you pay full attention to the matters one brings to you and that you are disciplined enough not to bring your agenda or spiritual interest to the matter.

And, like *Teaching for Discipleship* in general, this activity requires deep listening, prayerful sensitivity, and a truthful tongue. It helps to ask deep and powerful spiritual questions that quickly take someone below the surface nature of the matter and closer to the soulful nature of the matter.

KEEPING HEART

Finally, *Teaching for Discipleship*, like all vocational commitments, requires that we Keep Heart.

> We become teachers for reasons of the heart.
> But many of us lose heart as time goes by.
> How can we take heart, alone and together,
> so that we can give heart to our students and the world—
> which is what good teachers do.
> (Parker Palmer, *The Courage to Teach*)

Parker Palmer reminds us that we accept the call to teach because we are good-hearted people. And our ability to keep heart can be challenged, often seriously. His words can be adapted for those of us *Teaching for Discipleship*:

> We become ministers for reasons of the heart.
> Some of us lose heart as time goes by.
> How can we learn to *keep heart*, alone and together,
> so that we can give heart to our parishioners and to the world,
> which is what good ministers do.

In *Sustaining the Spirit: Callings, Commitments, and Vocational Challenges*, my wife, Catherine, lists several challenges putting our vocational commitments at risk. She offers several specific practices we can put in place in order to adapt to these challenges and sustain our callings. In my mind, there are a few in particular that can help those of us *Teaching for Discipleship* to Keep Heart.

The Ethic of the Enemy

Psychologists tell us that we unconsciously make enemies on purpose. That's right. We unconsciously create enemies because having an enemy benefits us in three ways.

First of all, when we make an enemy, the monkey of responsibility is off our back. Our vocational difficulty is not our fault. It's because of the enemy! Second, the Ethic of the Enemy helps us bond with colleagues. We get closer to each other when we stand against the enemy. We might not even talk a lot with a colleague unless the topic of the enemy comes up. Then we relate to each other in this sort of camaraderie or commiseration. Third, the Ethic of the Enemy helps us clarify our values. Having an enemy makes it easy for us to see how "I am so not like him/ her/them/that!" or "I totally disagree with his/her/their beliefs! I believe..."

So, while the Ethic of the Enemy helps us deflect responsibility, bond closer to co-workers, and clarify our values, it is a surefire way to lose heart. Contributing to the Ethic of the Enemy is like carrying kryptonite in our vocational backpack or handbag. You get weighed down by oppositional thinking, tension, animosity, suspicion, fear.

But its more than the weight of let's say, coal, or iron. It's poisonous. Carry the Ethic of the Enemy long enough and it will get inside you and poison the way you see things, hear things, do things. It's radioactive. It will make you bitter inside. We have all seen how the Ethic of the Enemy has made someone so bitter that they could no longer maintain a commitment to this ministry. We should confront injustice, inequity, meanness, and evil. In doing so, we practice testimony to what is right, excellent, noble, and true. But that's different than cultivating the Ethic of the Enemy.

Who's the enemy for us? Take your pick. We tend to say: "It's those dang parents, they drop off their kids and then they ... and how can we be successful when they ..." Or, "it's the pastor ... it's the bishop ... it's the Republicans ... it's the Democrats ... it's the media ... it's that movement ... it's the new DRE ... it's people from that school ... it's the liberals ... it's the conservatives ... it's ..."

Flick the remote on your television tonight and you will see that we now have a culture of the enemy. On one channel, someone says that this person or group is the enemy. Another channel has someone saying that someone else is the enemy.

I don't know if the Ethic of the Enemy will poison society with bitterness and animosity, etc., but it is a growing dynamic in Church work. All of us have seen the way it can poison one's ability to Keep Heart in this noble ministry of ours.

The practice of confession can help you disengage from the Ethic of the Enemy. Whether sacramental or otherwise, any good confession requires an examination:

How and when do we contribute to the Ethic of the Enemy by our language, our actions, our obsessions, our attitudes? Can we fess up to ourselves, to our colleagues and spouses, when we catch ourselves contributing to the Ethic of the Enemy?

It is more than recognizing how we contribute to the Ethic of the Enemy, it is the intentional effort to cut ourselves free from the crippling hold it has on us.

The Wisdom of the Ratio

Due to the increasing complexity involved in effective faith formation there is value in seeking the Wisdom of the Ratio. Dr.

Margaret Guider, a Franciscan nun and noted theologian at the Boston College School of Theology, first introduced me to this concept. She maintained that taking an either/or approach to ministry is not as helpful as it might have been in the past. Times are more complex. Faith formation is more and more complex in the face of dwindling resources, expanding learning needs, and a limited number of volunteers. Family configurations are more complex. Participation in parish life is more and more complex.

Instead of seeking to determine if either this or that is the best way to proceed, she suggests that it is much more helpful to seek the Wisdom of the Ratio:

> How often should I take this approach and how often should I take that approach?

> When should I stand up and when is it better to stay seated?

> How much time and energy should I invest in that?

> To what degree should I take care of other people's children and to what degree should I take care of my own children?

The land of And

We teach, lead, and serve a diverse group of believers. Some believers want this kind of devotion offered and some want this kind of social justice program offered. Some want a retreat to focus on this theme and some want a retreat that focuses on that theme. Some champion this point of view and some champion another point of view.

We cannot be everything to everyone. And we cannot betray the core beliefs and teachings of Christ and the Church. But we can try getting more comfortable living in the land of And instead of trying to keep at bay the spiritual and programmatic interests we don't resonate with.

Living in the land of And requires the willingness to respect and attend to a variety of Catholic spiritual interests and programs. The middle ground has moved. It is not as far on the left as some of us want it to be nor is it as far on the right as some of us want it to be.

We have not found the new middle yet. Living in the land of And will help you find it.

Finding it will help you Keep Heart.

Keeping Company

Closing the book here is fitting because the strongest way to Keep Heart just might be found in the practice of Keeping Company. Keeping Company refers to intentionally investing in relationships with a colorful collection of characters who understand your vocational lamentation, refrain from pouring syrupy spiritual clichés on it, and yet still have a way of reminding you why the ministry is still worth it.

This company of yours can be made up of individuals who don't even know one another, or even do the same work as you do.

The company I keep happens to be spread out across the country. It includes a couple in the Pacific Northwest. Whenever my travels take me to the West Coast, I try to add a travel segment that will bring me to their kitchen where we cook, share our vocational challenges, lament, and leave reassured that the work is still worth it.

The same goes for a friend of mine in southern Indiana, a basketball coach in Kentucky, my mom, two colleagues in Louisiana, and a theologian in Chicago who I keep company with via phone.

Keeping Company requires an intentional investment in a specific collection of relationships, all with a common *charism*, the ability to understand your vocational lamentation, and a way to remind you that it is still worth it.

This, unfortunately, may require you to quit Keeping Company with one or two individuals who, for one reason or more, operate out of the Ethic of the Enemy, fail to see the complexity of the work, or cannot acknowledge the need to hold the contradictions, paradox, and ambiguity that comes along with *Teaching for Discipleship*.

Whom do you need to be Keeping Company with? Stop Keeping Company with?

Cathy is fond of asking the echoing question: "Who may need you to be in the company they keep, and how open are you to doing so?"

At the end of a session on vocational callings and commitments at a conference for rising high school seniors, I was asked by the organizer to allow some time at the end for questions. One senior asked me to name the most memorable part of my own vocational life. I responded with something that was quite memorable: the four years I spent at Boystown working with the spiritual growth of those kids.

But as soon as I gave my answer, I *immediately* wanted a do-over. For as memorable as that Boystown experience was, it was not the best part of my vocational journey.

Then and there I made myself a promise that if the topic ever came up again, I would give the answer that rang most true for me.

Without a doubt, the best part of *Teaching for Discipleship* for me and for all of us, in the end and all along the way, is the company we get to keep.

For Reflection

What would you say is the dominant dimension of your spirituality these days — vertical, horizontal, or internal? What makes you say that?

Which one(s) would you like to cultivate when you get time?

Based on your experience, which seem to be the dominant dimension(s) among those you teach?

Do you think your program or your teaching emphasizes one dimension much more than the other(s)? What's the reason for your answer?

How and when could you focus on the other dimension(s) in your teaching?

For Reflection

This section lists 5 ways of mentoring or teaching informally:

Attending to Stories

Building Skills

Honoring Emotions

Offering Solidarity

Cultivating Spiritual Sensitivity

Which one best suits your personality and interest?

What is it about your ministry that comes closest to almost causing you to lose heart?

In light of this, how do you Keep Heart?

Which of these practices, if any, might help you Keep Heart?

Disconnecting the Ethic of the Enemy

Seeking the Wisdom of the Ratio

Living in the land of And

Keeping Company

For Reflection

Whom do you practice Keeping Company with?

Who might be asking you to be part of the company she or he keeps?

Now that you have finished this book, feel free to make yourself some notes here about *Teaching for Discipleship*.

Appendix

Current catechetical programs and resources are full of solid sessions. The two examples that follow are simply offered as illustrations through which we can compare inductive and deductive methodology.

Example 1:
Recognizing God's Presence

AN *INDUCTIVE* METHOD MIGHT PROCEED LIKE THIS:

Life Experience

All participants read the following quotes and discuss their answers in triads:

A college student studying biology says: "Studying the human birth process convinced me that there was a God. I mean, look at the way the human body was designed to produce more humans. The mother's body, like, automatically stops producing some regular stuff and automatically starts producing some new stuff just so she can nurture the baby. A whole, like, organized and complicated new process kicks in just to produce the baby. Afterward the process just automatically stops. Perfectly designed. Had to be invented by someone like God. Couldn't have been designed by accident, or, like, by itself."

A soldier in Iraq says: "War is about killing. Period. It's hell. Literally. Guys brutally trying to kill and mame each other.

Ruthless. It's the last place on earth that you'd expect to see God. But there is something really powerful — I'm gonna say holy, really — when you see someone sacrifice his or her life for another person, or sacrifice their life for the people of their country. On both sides. Whenever I saw it, I felt like I saw *true* love. Am I making any sense?"

Breaking news interrupts the TV show to report the devastation of a massive earthquake in China killing 50,000 people. After hearing the report, a high school sophomore stands up and heads to the fridge, saying: "I don't get it. How can God, who is supposed to be so loving and all, bring this on, like, 50,000 innocent people?"

- *Pick one of these statements and explain why you agree or disagree with it.*

- *Then offer another example to go along with the one you've picked.*

Faith Content

Through print, PowerPoint presentation, a textbook, or a hand-out participants are introduced to content regarding Ways of Coming to Know God (Truth, Beauty, Love) as found in the *Catechism* (31-36). The catechist takes them through this information, giving examples of each and checking for understanding along the way.

Response

Privately, or as a group, everyone responds to these kinds of questions:

- *When have you felt closest to God in the last six months?*

- *Was it during a certain activity, with a certain person or group, or in a certain place? Which?*

- *Write about a time when you recognized the Presence of God in a moment of Truth, Beauty, or Love. See if you can name a time for each of the three.*

- *What are the exact opposites of Truth, Beauty, Love?*

- *Can a person recognize the Presence of God in these times too? Explain your answer.*

A *DEDUCTIVE* APPROACH

might simply change the order of the process along with slightly different discussion questions:

Faith Content

Begin by introducing everyone to Ways of Coming to Know God (Truth, Beauty, Love) as found in the *Catechism* (31-36). The catechist takes the participants through this information, giving examples of each and checking for understanding along the way.

Life Experience

Everyone then reads the three quotes and discusses their answers in triads.

- *Pick one of these statements and explain why you agree or disagree with it.*

- *Then offer another example to go along with the one you've picked.*

Response

Privately, or as a group, everyone responds to these kinds of questions:

- *When have you felt closest to God in the last six months? Was it during a certain activity, with a certain person or group, or in a certain place? Which?*

- *Write about a time when you recognized the Presence of God in a moment of Truth, Beauty, or Love. See if you can name a time for each of the three.*

- *What are the exact opposites of Truth, Beauty, Love?*

- *Can a person recognize the Presence of God in these times too? Explain your answer.*

Example 2:
Righteous Anger,
or *Advocacy*

AN *INDUCTIVE* APPROACH

Life Experience

The catechist could share a newspaper story or a current event in which a person or group is displaying righteous anger as a form of advocacy for injustice.

OR

Participants would be asked — privately or in groups — to describe a time they were angry over something they felt was unjust, or when they saw someone being taken advantage of and how they responded to that situation.

Faith Content

The Scripture passage of Jesus and the money-changers in the Temple would be studied followed by some background information that would clarify the reason their presence in the Temple was infuriating back in Jesus' day.

And supplemental discussion questions might include:

- *Who or what reminds you of money-changers in our society today?* (unfair lenders/mortgage companies, health insurance companies, frauds taking advantage of the elderly, anonymous Internet rumormongers, etc.)

- *What might Jesus suggest as an appropriate way to respond? What would advocacy look like in this situation?*

- *How can someone be guilty of unjust advocacy?*

Response

Everyone would then be asked to privately self-assess:

"Give yourself a grade regarding your overall tendency to engage in advocacy and list two political or personal situations that you are willing to pay more attention to."

A *DEDUCTIVE* METHOD

would invert the order of the first two steps and look like this:

Faith Content

Start with the Scripture passage of Jesus and the money-changers in the Temple followed by some background information that would clarify the reason their presence in the Temple was infuriating back in Jesus' day.

Life Experience

Everyone would then be asked — privately or in groups — to describe a time they were angry over something they felt was unjust or when they saw someone being taken advantage of.

OR

Share a newspaper story or a current event in which a person or group is displaying righteous anger as a form of advocacy for injustice — much like Jesus did in the Scripture passage.

Supplemental discussion questions might include:

- *Who or what reminds you of money-changers in our society today?* (unfair lenders/mortgage companies, health insurance companies, frauds taking advantage of the elderly, anonymous Internet rumormongers, etc.)

- *What might Jesus suggest as an appropriate way to respond? What would advocacy look like in this situation?*

- *How can someone be guilty of unjust advocacy?*

Response

Everyone would then be asked to privately self-assess:

"Give yourself a grade regarding your overall tendency to engage in advocacy and list two political or personal situations that you are willing to pay more attention to."

Options: If you have a sixty-minute session:

A. You could divide the session into three different topics and use the inductive method with some topic(s) and the deductive method with some topic(s). If you spent only fifteen minutes on each topic, you could use the remaining fifteen minutes in the session for a closing prayer experience related to the three topics covered in the session. Covering several topics in a session often keeps the pace moving and keeps interest from waning. Prayer done well can touch some candidates in ways that inductive and deductive methods do not, especially at night, or with music, a candle, and Bibles.

OR

B. Both inductive and deductive methods connect the same three components. But you are free to spend more time on one component than the others. You may, for example, spend twenty minutes on the first component, thirty minutes on the second, and ten minutes on the third.

SO...

When you look for catechetical resources:

- keep an eye out for how often they employ these two different methods;

- see if it enables you to fit several topics into one session, using different techniques;

- determine if the suggested questions, activities, and information best addresses the content you want to address — and are within the comprehension level of your participants.

Note: The examples above are derived from the Cornerstone Series (for high schools) by Our Sunday Visitor.